Gabriel Pomerand

Saint Ghetto of the Loans: Grimoire

Amplified Edition

translated from French by
Michael Kasper and Bhamati Viswanathan

WORLD POETRY

Saint Ghetto of the Loans: Grimoire

Published with the permission of Garance Pomerand

Orignally published as *Saint ghetto des prêts: grimoire* (Paris: O.L.B., [1950]). An earlier version of the translation was published by Ugly Duckling Presse in 2006, in Brooklyn, NY, as #1 in UDP's Lost Literature Series.

Amplified Edition, First Printing, 2023
ISBN 978-1-954218-13-0

World Poetry Books
New York, NY
www.worldpoetrybooks.com

Distributed in the US by SPD/Small Press Distribution
www.spdbooks.org

Distributed in the UK and Europe by Turnaround Publisher Services
www.turnaround-uk.com

Library of Congress Control Number: 2023931092

Cover art by Gabriel Pomerand
Hand-lettering by Michael Kasper
Cover design by Andrew Bourne
Typesetting by Don't Look Now
Printed in Lithuania by BALTO print

World Poetry Books is committed to publishing exceptional translations of poetry from a broad range of languages and traditions, bringing the work of modern masters, emerging voices, and pioneering innovators from around the world to English-language readers in affordable trade editions. Founded in 2017, World Poetry Books is a 501(c)(3) nonprofit and charitable organization based in New York City, and affiliated with the Humanities Institute and the Translation Program at the University of Connecticut (Storrs).

Table of Contents

Saint ghetto des prêts
grimoire
de
gabriel pomerand

This book is dedicated to
ROXANE POMERAND
who patiently supported the construction of this puzzle
even as she discovered a new form of embroidery.

The map at the beginning of this work is by Monsieur M. JACNO,
and was taken from "La légende de Saint germain des prés"
(éditions de la Roulotte, Paris).

Preface

This book is made up of signs that say just what they are.
There's no mystery. That's the whole mystery.

These little compositions form beautiful pages of writing—like early books, with their serpentine letters—they make for a luxurious puzzle. These pages are rooted in books that can be read, symbolically, even when closed.

He's talking to himself. He'll say to one: *I am silent*; to another: *idiot.*

A disciple addresses this prayer to his dying master: Give me the secret of wisdom. The old man answers: *never think about the crocodile.* Then he dies.

—What was he trying to say? the disciple asks himself, and for decades he keeps coming back to the same question in his mind. The hour of his death approaches. *Never think about the crocodile.* And he's done nothing but think about it for twenty years......

On page one of one of his books, Pomerand has written: To Madame So-and-So, *no comment.*

Those who opened the cover could hear a chuckle that spoke volumes about what was on display within their souls. He, however, thought he'd ruled out any misunderstanding.

To sum up some hard-to-express contradictions, we're in the habit of citing the following funerary anecdote: *my tears won't bring her back to me, and that's why I cry.*

His original plan was to fabricate easy signs. That got caught in its own trap and they were made to sing. Poets who resist being dazzled by phrases do it all the time. We blame contemporary literature for its automatism,* but there's little we see opposing it, except theories so tattered as to be worth less than all the automatisms.

This grimoire represents a safety catch for the verbiage.

I believe in a scientific division of roles in society—with its motorcoaches, tarot cards, and law courts. There are people who are born to have meaning. They are deciphered, or attacked.

This little tree of myths that is Pomerand, born to be read every which way, even when he's composing cantatas of howls and parables shaped like buttocks or soup spoons, seems to me full of meaning.

As for the ghetto that he stylizes in this work, we know it's dead and incinerated herein, unless Pomerand is a pallbearer for the thousands of pilgrims who come every evening to park their cars there.

Jacques BARATIER.

---

* Automatopoeism, as Pomerand says.

Introduction

This book is unusual and immobile, yet orderly as a caste. I'd love it if, in the future, the organic world showed such an icy face, impassive and tough.

We're the new egyptians.

Everywhere, people are building pyramids.

I dream of a book of mysteries equal to the arrogance and serenity in faces carved on pharaohs' mummies.

From nothingness, I've dug out each of the signs that make up this work, like one obliged to invent wisdom. Impassive Brahmin, thus do I picture my potential and future reader.

It will be necessary to work through a series of procedures before turning the corner; to climb from hierarchy to hierarchy until attaining the center.

Geometric priestliness, or the dream of a clear and obscure style.

It's not necessary that writing be window-paned, but featherbrained ... and it is necessary to tie things up.

It's necessary that style be tightly wrapped in searing penetration.

It's necessary that there be modern locks for the senses' strongboxes.

It's necessary that meanings be covered with fifty lids and hatches, and open sesames be lost within.

I wish my mind could steer clear of its certifiable miseries.

I wish to dress splendidly, and in this sense, no doubt, I have *an artistic soul*, in an obscenely simple century.

I wish one put on clothes to make love.
I aim to abandon the pampas and settle in a rocky place.
I'll carve in stone a new way of writing made for stones.

I don't like modern literature—anyway, no one does.

It's too precise at the outset; in the end too vague, and dancing before our eyes.

I wish it was more indefinite and more precise, that is, just what it isn't.

I wish its content were closer to what matters, to the stockpile of vital forces within its signs.

I start by tossing out my school-fed illusions, by shaking off and—who knows—shaking up the smug poise of ordinary meanings. I disarm.

Afterwards, I gather myself in each of my cracks.

Actually, I arm myself to the teeth.

Buried in the temple it built for itself, my mind marches around in impervious armor, a great big *de-braining device*.

I have to say it was Isou who set loose this new phenomenon that manifests as my understanding, and ever since I've kept it off course and out of the race.

It's been five years since we wandered the streets together, deep in debate, and he filled my head with a mess of ideas in which the surprise of youthful poetry, of theater, of erotology, of philosophy, of *metagraphics*, and perhaps, one day, of medicine, was expressed succinctly, too fast and mixed up for me to grasp anything except that which thrilled me the most: verse.

But, *metagraphics*, I came to it, in reality, as something I could do right away, as a necessary extension of my spiritual state, as my normal code of conduct.

While leafing through old magic manuals and luxurious incunables I'd longed for much vaster precision, for the chance to re-create terms excluded from current writing.

Who hasn't dreamt of inventing each of his words, of giving himself at least apparently, if not inwardly, the illusion of creating things?

No doubt Isou made me a sign once, in the course of I no longer know what lost morning, but not only have I alone made my work, but also all my tools, focusing especially on research for a system of intrinsic figuration.

I've tried in my turn to model the figurative essence of creation, and this glove in which a writer signs personally for the people of his times.

This mask I've given myself in eternity's comedy, it alone will earn me gasps from spectators as I advance enfolded in my cape of ink and night.

I absolutely don't want to use pictograms except in the absolute case where drawing will best express the revealed order.

In any case, I've tried to replace a debased, dried up symbolism—that of words—with a new symbolism, torn from the flesh of acquired ideas.

The visual poet becomes an essential part of the woodwork of figuration.

Writing is an anthropometric measurement thanks to which one recognizes types.

The substance remains, then, above all a problem of photography, which caresses evil even as it shows it as it is.

We're no longer beating around the bush.

There's no thesis in this text where each thing *is*.

There'll be neither summons here, nor threat, but an economic division, a savings, leading things toward their inevitable expenditure.

I have no mercy on my habits.

Sworn disqualifications scour words, as if pitiless acid were to destroy the beloved's face, obliging me to reconstruct for her, surgically, a more beautiful, more fitting expression.

What will no doubt strike the reader, at first, when considering the pictograms in this work, will be the geometric deliberateness of the images.

I allowed myself no freedom in these expressions, as if contempt for my self and its weakness could perfect the quest for solemnity.

The prestige of the prophetic derives from its supernatural aspect.

For all that is divine is perfect.

I don't have to show anyone the lewd trembling inside me—inside anyone.

I'd like to build, instead of temples, a temple-writing.

Sumptuousness is always so proud.

I love pomp and opulence.

I believe, tomorrow, pictography will be very opulent.

And I'd love to be part of its pomp.

In any case, I've always kept the difficult and luxurious parts for myself, fearing generosity and enthusiasm, or desiring harmony among traits, like delicate flute phrases that can snare serpents in their nets.

In art it's necessary to doubt the first glance, especially in art that calls for one.

But for the first time, I've fooled with the view.

I want to work the miracle that is precisely the act whereby one comes to *no longer believe one's own eyes.*

I halve my steps as if to fool the obvious.

There's some higher zone of art that exists, or one of intelligence, or sensibility.

Now, here, the first trait is musical, because it has to please; the second is logical, intelligible.

I started with a written text that I wanted to cover and clothe.

But beneath these many robes, monstrously clad, a woman of flesh and bone—for whatever she's worth—lurks.

What I mean is that a clear concept binds the fragments of this primitive fantasy, exactly as an architect's concept coalesces in the chaos of laying foundations.

Sensory confusion isn't worth it, except as part of a profound victory over the self.

I don't care about current events because their hold on us is so superficial, for they only speak of what's immediate, of superfluous things they aim to break or re-make.

But I recognize each of their words in newspapers I no longer read, where all these decayed terms linger still.

Moreover, I don't want a mere transformation of syntax, but a morphological spasm.

The circulation of expressions in sentences and phrases, their inversions and combinations, now seem ridiculous to me.

I'd like to be able to reflect on each and every word.

I'd like not only to give each one a different subterranean meaning, but also to break its jaw and thus transform the face it apparently pretends to possess forever.

I've tried to sink my claws into the belly of an idea so as to retrieve each term from its guts right from the start.

I hope this book's morphology borrows means from interior modes of writing and from diverse other manners to better expose its inner workings, the digestive system of the organism.

Moreover, I don't insist too much on diverse means, for they're as varied as the universe of graphics.

What's essential is to not live on what's inherited, to not accept ill-gotten gains, and to ponder the potential for other, richer meanings.

What's essential is to reflect on each of these expressions and to find substitutes that go beyond an illustrated Larousse.

I want it understood that only the avant-garde of intelligence itself preoccupies me, and not at all the schools this avant-garde fits into.

I dread the day when the name of an invention—which is a phenomenon of commodification—overshadows the real search for transgression.

I love perpetual effort and risk of every kind, whether it is fighting against rules or against the nature of things.

Throughout my life, I've had no other goal than to be an extremist, at that battlefront which alarm clocks suggest even as they lure us into the traps of life.

Paris, July 1950.
G.P.

Notes:

Jacques Baratier (1918–2009), film-maker with whom Pomerand collaborated on the movie *Disorder*.

Isidore Isou (real name Jean-Isidore Goldstein, 1925-2007), chief Lettrist theorist, poet, etc.

See the Afterword for more information on Pomerand's associates.

Saint Ghetto of the Loans

Saint germain des prés is a ghetto.

All there wear yellow stars on their hearts.

It's Cocteau's star, which is a cocktail of stars.

Saint germain des prés holds a mirror to heaven.

Saint germain des prés est un ghetto.

Chacun y porte une étoile jaune sur le coeur.

C'est l'étoile de Cocteau qui est un cocktail d'étoiles.

Saint germain des prés est un miroir pour le ciel.

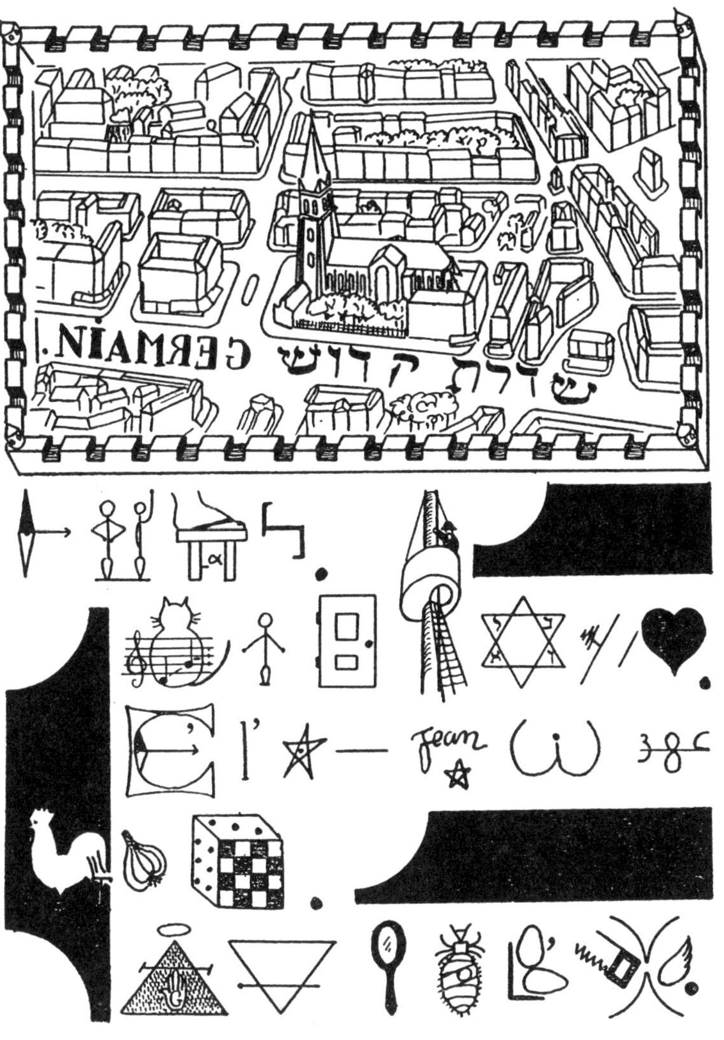
Jean

Everyone finds there a star capsized within their souls.

What's more, Cocteau's cocktail is sour, like essence of castor.

It stinks from his patchouli around here, Cocteau, vintage nineteen hundred.

Tonight, a pederast offered me a cocktail, proposing that we chat man to man.

I refused, considering

Tout homme y déniche un astre chaviré dans son âme.

Le cocktail de Cocteau a d'ailleurs une acidité d'eau de ricin.

Cela pue son patchouli par ici, c'est du Cocteau mille neuf cent.

Cette nuit, un pédéraste désirait m'offrir un cocktail, me proposant de discuter d'homme à homme.

J'ai refusé, considérant

tre
Jean
ClNa
Jean
19
00.

that, with him, one could hardly converse man to woman.

I'm distressed to be discussing such absurdities, but there are these psychoanalytical burps in my subconscious that drift about and express themselves, sometimes, in the guise of bad wordplay.

Saint germain des prés is a neighborhood in Paris, where girls come nightly to be

qu'avec lui, on ne pouvait guère parler que d'homme à femme.

Je suis navré de dire des absurdités, mais dans mon subconscient, il y a des rots psychanalytiques, qui se promènent et s'expriment parfois sous forme de mauvais calembours.

Saint germain des prés est un quartier de Paris, où les filles viennent la nuit, pour se

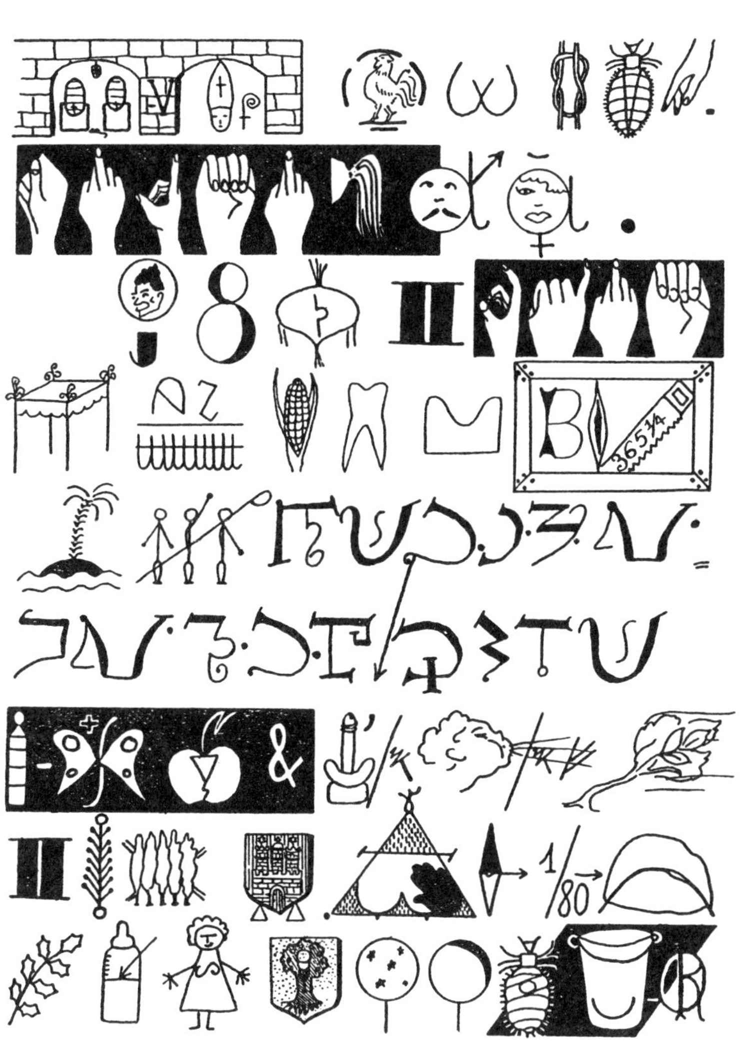

raped, where every man yearns to deflower life.

Life and the girls return home virgins, flowers between their legs, for we're a generation whose men, having stood erect too often in the recent war, have lately drooped.

My neighborhood is an island swimming in the Seine, which

faire violer, où chaque homme veut dépuceler la vie.

La vie et les filles s'en retournent pucelles, la fleur entre les jambes, car nous sommes une génération, dont les hommes, ayant trop fait la queue au cours de la récente guerre, l'ont perdue ce jourd'hui.

Mon quartier est une île qui nage sur la Seine, et qui

100
80

cries for help with a jazz tune.

xxxxx xxxx[1] *is a lovable heart, a satyr, they say, who has however satyrized only his wife, thus hatching two brats.*

But he was a hero of fantasy.

In Paris, a Black is a White who doesn't rape.

Here, as if in a game of checkers, everyone can land on a different square, and dealing in

crie au secours sur un air de jazz.

xxxxx xxxx est un cardiaque aimable réputé satyre, et qui n'a pourtant satyrisé que sa femme, pondant ainsi deux marmots.

Mais ce fut un héros de fantasie.

A Paris un noir est un blanc qui ne viole pas.

Ici, ainsi que dans un jeu de dames chacun peut tomber sur des carrés différents, et les données de

flesh is dealing at poker.

Everyone can change color next time.

Saint germain des prés is a drowned drunk peacefully floating from one bridge to another.

It's a mushroom vomited from fever and Fargue's lamp.

All the streetlamps are Americans.

When one bumps the lampposts, they prattle in

peau sont des données de poker.

Chacun pourra changer de couleur la fois prochaine.

Saint germain des prés est un ivrogne noyé qui flotte paisiblement d'un pont à un autre.

C'est un champignon vomi par la fièvre et la lampe de Fargue.

Tous les réverbères sont des Américains.

Quand on coudoie les lampadaires, ils dégoisent en

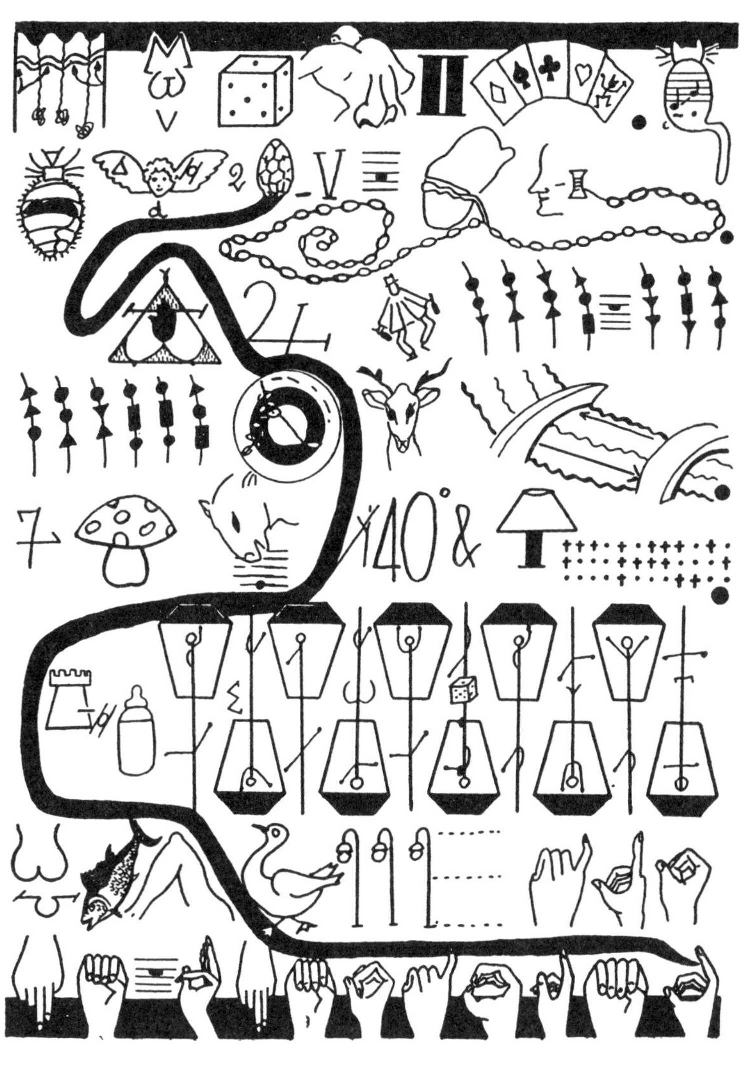

yankee.

As if drunk, I feel displaced, stumbling into gas jets that batter me with dictionaries from perfidious Albion.

All redskins wear war medals around their necks.

They're either the colorful butterfly cocoons or the flypaper which give Saint germain des prés its air of a miniscule cemetery.

The neighborhood's mandarin is xxxxxxx xxxxxxx,[2] *though there's also his neological pekinese.*

There's also the man with the decomposed

yankee.

Comme ivrogne, je me sens dépaysé, en butant aux becs de gaz, qui me cabossent en usant des dictionnaires de la perfide Albion.

Tous les peaux-rouges portent des croix de guerre au cou.

Ce sont des noeuds-papillons multicolores, ou des papiers tue-mouches qui donnent à Saint germain des prés son air de cimetière minuscule.

Le mandarin du quartier est xxxxxxx xxxxxxx mais c'est aussi son pékinois néologique.

C'est aussi l'homme à la sansonnette

songbird and a skirt-chaser, dressed up Haarlem-style.

At the bistro where I work there's a fat lady who grins at me with all the veins of gold in Colorado or the Klondike.

She crossed the Ocean so as to be raped by Boris Vian, whom she believed to be the terrible Black from "I Spit on Your

dégénérée et un trousseur de jupes du style Haarlem.

Au bistrot où je travaille est une grosse dame qui me sourit avec tous les filons d'or du Colorado et du Klondyke.

Elle traversa l'Océan, pour se faire violer par Boris Vian qu'elle croit être le terrible noir de «j'irai cracher dans vos

Spitoons

Dancing After a Dog's Coffin."[3]

xxxxx xxxx, xxxx of a current Kobra, scorpion man.[4]

xxxx-xxxx xxxxxx[5] *has a cockeyed view of the world, an oblique weltanschauung.*

When little, he'd stuck his finger in his eye, and ever since he's had an odd view of philosophy.

Having swallowed his toothpicks, that gave him a fragrant taste of the universe.

crachoirs

dansant derrière un cercueil de chien».

xxxxx xxxx, xxxxx de Kobra actuel, l'homme au scorpion.

xxxx-xxxx xxxxxx a une déviation louche du monde, un weltanschauung oblique.

Petit, il s'est mis le doigt dans l'oeil, et depuis il a une vision curieuse de la philosophie.

Ayant avalé son cure-dents, cela lui a donné un goût aromatique de l'univers.

It's existentialist acid coming direct from Quasimodo the Asymmetric.

I knew a woman who gave birth to a devil.

He was called the devil of xxxxxxx[6] *or the extra sex of existentialism.*

For references, xxxxxxxxx xxxxxx[7] *has noble titles and numerous credentials, proving him an illustrious friend for the redhead xxxxxxx dixit xxxx-xxxxx,*[8] *grand niece*

C'est l'acide existentialiste arrivant en ligne droite de Quasimodo l'asymétrique.

J'ai connu une femme qui accoucha d'un diable.

On l'appela le diable de xxxxxxx ou le sexe surnuméraire de l'existentialisme.

xxxxxxxxx xxxxxx a pour références, titres de noblesse et lettres de créances cumulés, d'être l'illustre ami de la rousse xxxxxxx dixit xxxx-xxxxx, petite nièce

of a man who, for references, noble titles, and accumulated credentials, has only his having been the illustrious friend of Mallarmé dixit Stéphane.

She doesn't exist, except through her references.

She's a link between two or three beings.

She doesn't exist.

She's an imaginary point, a mathematical point mistaken for a commodity.

One says of her what one says of a geometric figure:

In place of a square, suppose we take xxxx[9]

d'un homme qui n'avait pour références, titres de noblesse et lettres de créances cumulés qu'été l'illustre ami de Mallarmé dixit Stéphane.

Elle n'existe que par ses références.

Elle est un rapport entre deux ou trois êtres.

Elle n'existe pas.

Elle est un point imaginaire, un point mathématique pris pour commodité.

On dit d'elle ce qu'on dit d'une figure géométrique:

Au lieu d'un carré supposons que nous ayons xxxx

Стефан

xxxxx xxxxxxx.[10]

Flat as a board, he has teeth like nails.

When xxxxxx[11] *sleeps on xxxx-xxxxx he's in training to be a fakir.*

He'll appear soon onscreen as the-man-who-sleeps-on-a-bed of nails.

xxxxx[12] *is a girl who hides her hatching.*

She must have a roulette wheel between her thighs for, with her, one plays a losing game.

Don't approach her

xxxxx xxxxxxx.

Plat comme une planche, il a des dents en tête de clous.

Le jour où xxxxxx couche sur xxxx-xxxxx il fait un entraînement de fakir.

Il apparaîtra bientôt sur l'écran dans l'homme - qui - couche - sur - une - planche à clous.

xxxxx est une fille qui cache sa ponte.

Elle doit avoir une roulette entre les cuisses, car, avec elle, on joue perdant.

Il ne faut pas trop

too often, for, when her fur's bristling, one sees she's expert in all kinds of jiu-jitsu.

I saw her break the bones of a little neighborhood pimp, and wring his dick, which shouldn't get mixed up with what's called the Mound of Venus.

On viewing her rump, one frequently wants to mix up her back side with her front, suggesting

l'approcher, car, à son poil hérissé, on voit qu'elle est championne de toutes les espèces de jiu-jitsu.

Je l'ai vue broyer des os à un petit maquereau du quartier, et lui garroter la queue, qu'il ne faut pas incorporer à ce qu'on appelle la bosse de l'amour.

En voyant son arrière-train on a souvent envie d'incorporer son envers à son endroit, alléguant

that she could put pasties on her ass and makeup on her headband.

xxxxxxxx[13] *is boss in the Saint germain des prés xxxx,*[14] *which is a kind of peoples' potty.*

I'm speaking of the xxxx, not of xxxxxxxx, he being just the boss.

There, one sees sundry shitheads, training themselves to fart like sparklers.

xxxxxxxx is very proud of his ritzy pals.

At Tabou, where he once held court, one comes across the Aga-Khan,

qu'elle pourrait mettre un cache-nichons à ses fesses et se farder le bibi.

xxxxxxxx est le patron du xxxx Saint germain des prés qui est une espèce de tinette populaire.

Je parle du xxxx, non de xxxxxxxx, lui, n'étant que le patron.

On y voit maints merdeux s'entraîner à péter du bougie-bougie.

xxxxxxxx est très fier de ses connaissances mondaines.

Au Tabou, où il officiait jadis, on croise l'Aga-Khan,

his wife, Mahatma Gandhi, and other suckers, to whom xxxxxxxx salaamed so much that ever since he's been a belly dance master, such that his belly's never empty.

Monsieur xxxxx[15] *is a man to whom his own nose seems a stranger.*

He's the man with the best-selling plague.

He's a rebel at Gallimard Press every day, from nine o'clock

sa femme, Mahatma Gandhi et d'autres têtes de turcs, auxquels xxxxxxxx faisait tant de salamalecs, qu'il est depuis passé maître dans la danse du ventre qu'il ne faut pas incorporer à la danse devant le buffet.

Monsieur xxxxx est un homme qui a le nez étranger à soi-même.

C'est l'homme à la peste best-seller.

C'est un révolté des éditions Gallimard tous les jours de neuf heures

مهتما
جاندي
سلام
عليكم

'til noon and from two o'clock 'til six, except on days when he's on the lecture circuit, where pretty little plague victims listen, enraptured and insistent.

Monsieur xxxxxxx xxxx, Jean,[16] *even as he's stroked by its women, swims through the neighborhood on his way to the Champs-Elysées*

à midi et de quatorze heures à dix-huit heures, indépendamment des jours où il est en tournée de conférences, et où de petits pestiférés bien mignons l'écoutent radieusement et invinciblement.

Monsieur xxxxxx xxxx, Jean, ainsi qu'il se fait apeloter par les femmes traverse le quartier à la nage pour aller vers les Champs-Elysées

or Pigalle, a book always underarm, the one wounded wing remaining from some sort of flight. He's as commanding as his beard, he'd taken care to hide it between his legs so as to pass unnoticed. He comes down from the Pantheon and, in death, forgot to speak. Because he speaks badly in any language other than the onomatopoeic

ou Pigalle, toujours un livre sous le bras, l'unique aile blessée qui lui soit restée d'une sorte de vol. Il fait tant maître que sa barbe, il a pris soin de la cacher entre ses jambes pour passer incognito. Il descend du Panthéon, et, dans la mort, il a oublié de parler. Car il parle mal un autre langage qu'onomatopéique

official neighborhood tongue. He appears to be hoping for a speedy return to places where mummies mildew.

The amazing xxxxxx xxxxxxx[17] *supports his pinhead on a reed's stem.*

Foreseeing him, his father François grew fond of Pascal's thinking reed.

xxxxxx xxxxxxx is a worm who tilts up like an obelisk and believes himself en-

verbiage officiel du quartier. Il paraît espérer un retour prochain vers les lieux où les momies moisissent.

L'émerveillant xxxxxx xxxxxxx maintient sa tête d'épingle sur un os de roseau.

C'est en le pressentant que son père François, aima le roseau pensant de Pascal.

xxxxxx xxxxxxx est un asticot qui se balance tout droit comme une verge en obélisque et se croit défini-

sconced in an inner ante-room of politics.

He's an undertaker's assistant who likes André Malraux and lacks the hypocrisy of skeletons.

When he undresses, one can't help but see he's a heap of bones, brought and bound together with a wire rim.

He's as skeletal as de Gaulle and about as imperious.

tivement dans une prochaine antichambre de la politique.

C'est un croquemort qui aime André Malraux et n'a pas l'hypocrisie des squelettes.

Lorsqu'il se déshabillote on doit voir qu'il est un amoncellement d'os réunis et concentrés par une lunette.

Il est aussi squelettique que de Gaulle et est aussi tribun que lui.

Oh! my neighborhood, my neighborhood, you stink so of shrimp,

One might be in Marseilles.

It's the point of intersection for all the anarchists who have millions in the United States and have come over here to play pickpockets, and

Oh! mon quartier, mon quartier, comme tu pues la crevette,

On s'en croirait à Marseille.

C'est le point d'intersection de tous les anarchistes qui ont des millions aux Etats-Unis et ont débarqué ici pour jouer les faucheux, et

H²OH,(
1/80)×
100
1000
000

for all the millionaires whose pockets are full of dreams, and who've already built castles beneath the bridges of the Seine whence the spirit of the universe watches over everything.

The white queen's queers, when meeting up to make a date, talk taboo or toptaboo.

And if my spurts

de tous les millionnaires qui ont les poches pleines de rêves, et ont déjà bâti quelques châteaux sous les ponts de la Seine d'où veille tout l'esprit de l'univers.

Les pédales de la reine blanche, en se rencontrant pour se donner rendez-vous se disent tabou ou tapobou.

Et si mes saillies

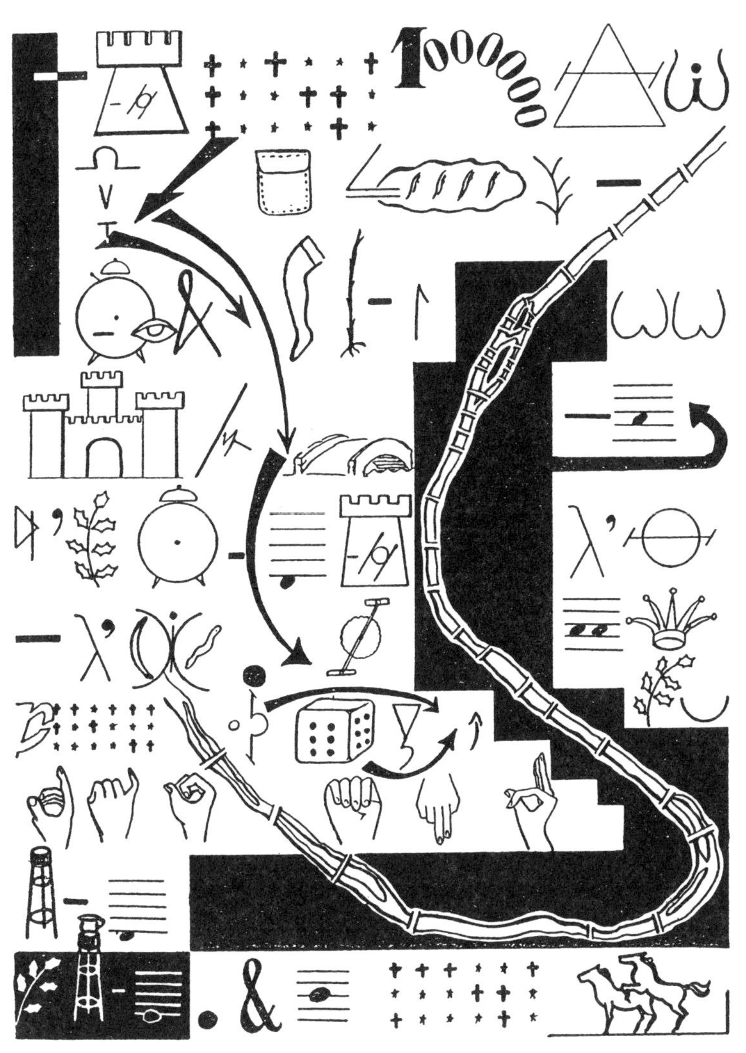

have whiskers, that's because they come from a very old and very noble family.

Hollywood should move to Saint germain des prés where there's a world of love affairs;

From Los Angeles, which lingers in dangling doorways of slumber, and where all the men fiddle alone like the solitary heroes

ont de la barbe, c'est parce qu'elles sont d'une très vieille et très noble famille.

C'est à Saint germain des prés qu'Hollywood devrait s'installer, car c'est un monde d'affaires de coeur;

Via Los-Angelès qui passe par ces portiques suspendus de sommeil, et où tous les hommes se baguenaudent solitaires comme les héros individualisés

× 1000
II
IX
H_2O

of the screen.

There is no Saint germain des prés. There are only spirits who survey the streets of terraced terraces awaiting the occurrence of unique events.

Every film is marvelously unique, and that's why, after the end, the heroes find themselves cuckolded and unha

de l'écran.

Il n'y a pas de Saint germain des prés. Il n'y a que des génies qui arpentent les rues de terrasses en terrasses, attendant des éventualités singulières pour se manifester.

Tout film est une singulière merveille, et c'est pourquoi après la fin, les héros se découvrent cocus et malhe

ppy. They're no longer tied to the selves they've presented.

These shadows are unfaithful to their canvas.

The natives of Saint germain des prés are cuckolds who smash their icons while on the lookout for tragic accidents.

In their eyes, a lone woman passing by is a prospect of death who strolls and slices though the landscape.

Every woman is a goodbye kiss and a "happy end."

ureux. Ils n'ont plus par rapport à quoi se montrer.

Ce sont des ombres infidèles à leur toile.

Les indiogènes de Saint germain des prés sont des cocus qui choquent leurs images aux aguets d'accidents terribles.

Une seule femme qui passe, sous leurs yeux est une perspective de mort qui déambule et tranche le paysage.

Toute femme est un baiser d'adieu et un happy end.

To prove themselves, women need men. They're masturbated, always ready to pay men to discover within them the revelation of their very own mystery, for they'd like to be mysterious, so as to be worthy of their own imaginations.

Thus are goddesses resuscitated, in this open-air temple, like a man respectful of his own greatness, who salutes himself while managing

Les femmes ont nécessité d'hommes pour se prouver. Elles sonts des masturbées qui seraient prêtes à rémunérer des hommes pour découvrir en eux la révélation de leur mystère personnel, car elles se veulent mystérieuses pour être dignes de leur imagination personnelle.

Ainsi sont ressuscitées les déesses, dans ce temple découvert, comme un homme respectueux de sa grandeur personnelle, et qui se salue en se tirant

to tip his hat.

All the prophets have cleared out, and all the gods have lyres but no public to talk to, sweet merchants of cut-rate smut and amiable nights, just twenty years old.

How sweet to subsist in a world which is falling apart.

They have a cult of the everyday banality of excitement.

Installed in despair as if in

un coup de chapeau.

Tous les prophètes sont déserts, et tous les dieux ont des lyres mais n'ont pas de public auquel parler, doux marchands de pouasie au rabais et de nuits affables qui ont encore vingt ans.

Qu'il est doux de subsister dans un monde qui s'écroule.

Ils ont le culte de la banalité quotidienne de l'exaltant.

Installés dans le désespoir comme dans

an all-weather street stall, I tell them they'll be bankrupt before long.

In the hall of the scholarly societies, some ladies, selected by design by the good lord to believe in predestination, come every week to hear how the end of the world is due tomorrow.

They have such

un éventaire de quatre-saisons, je leur annonce qu'ils feront faillite d'ici peu.

A la salle des sociétés savantes, des dames choisies à dessein par le bon dieu pour croire à la prédestination, viennent chaque semaine entendre que la fin du monde est pour demain.

Elles ont encore

a short time to live, yet they're still available to observe others' deaths.

These are little old monsters with a tidy air, who ask one another to tea on Saturday afternoons, and actually read the bible.

They smell of pee, Church, and jam jars.

I have a friend who'll say anything in order to stay open-minded.

He's a gambler trapped in his folly by a zipper, who strips day

si peu à vivre, qu'elles sont disponibles pour voir aussi la mort des autres.

Ce sont de vieux petits monstres à l'air propret, que s'invitent à prendre le thé, le samedi après-midi, et qui lisent vraiment la bible.

Elles sentent le pipi, l'église, et les pots de confiture.

J'ai un ami qui dit n'importe quoi pour se garder ouvert.

C'est un joueur vérouillé dans sa folie par une fermeture éclair, et qui se dépossède jour

after day like the pooets do, so he can believe himself richer.

When he feels like committing suicide, he bursts into tears at the thought of such misery and gives himself another year to live.

That's gone on for twenty years.

While waiting, to prepare himself for the approaching infinitude, he lets his beard grow.

With this beard he gains in patience what he loses in fragility.

The Church of Saint germain des prés is the only savage in the neighborhood.

No words are tender enough to

nellement comme les pouètes, pour se croire plus riche.

Lorsqu'il veut se suicider, il pleure un grand coup sa misère et s'accorde encore une dernière année de vie.

Cela dure depuis vingt ans.

En attendant, pour s'entraîner au prochain infini, il laisse pousser sa barbe.

Avec sa barbe, il gagne en patience ce qu'il perd en fragilité.

L'Eglise de Saint germain des prés est l'unique sauvage du quartier.

Aucun mot n'est assez tendre pour

describe

how her bell pillages heaven.

How she bows her head, like a lover in the evening, to hear all the urchins pay court; migrating from her memory into the present, like a sea horse, and galloping while fear mounts all around, ahead of the inflexible fifth centenary.

Returning each morning with

décrirc

comme son clocher pille le ciel.

Comme elle courbe le tête, telle une amoureuse le soir, pour entendre tous les voyous lui faire la cour; émigrée de sa mémoire dans le contemporain, comme un cheval de la mer, et galopant tandis que la peur monte autour, devant la cinq centenaire impérissable.

Retournant chaque matin avec

the roosters and the paperboys, to the same discreet spot where the last lovers still arrange dates, never leaving to chance the chore of deciding where to meet, the last lovers of the tertiary period make a date with the bus.

The church of Saint germain des prés isn't afraid of the atom bomb, discovered by those same Americans who

les coqs et les vendeurs de journaux, au même endroit sage où les derniers amoureux se fixent encore des rendez-vous, et ne laissant pas au hasard, le soin de déterminer l'emplacement des rencontres, les derniers amoureux de l'ère tertiaire se donnent rendez-vous avec l'autobus.

L'église de Saint germain des prés n'a pas peur de la bombe atomique découverte par les mêmes américains qui

come to pray on its bosom, though it's the devil's work.

The church of Saint germain des prés is the museum of shadows.

One Christmas night a drunk, a great friend of mine, mistook the church for a music hall and went inside for a quick fuck.

The priest called a police officer.

The drunk swore he'd find the good lord and give him a thrashing.

Only a church that had

viennent prier en son sein, est cependant une oeuvre du diable.

L'église de Saint germain des prés est le musée des ombres.

Un soir de Noël, un ivrogne, un grand ami à moi, a pris l'église pour un beuglant et y est entré tirer un coup en accéléré.

L'abbé a appelé un agent de police.

L'ivrogne s'est juré de rencontrer le bon dieu pour lui filer une dérouillée.

Seule l'église qui a

watched its adolescence sell out could accept the selling off of its dignity without flinching.

The virgins hereabouts carry inside themselves a promise of decrepitude masked beneath a sneer.

They've nicked the grimace from the murderer at the streetcorner, famine's knife between his teeth, who's waiting for some two-legged wallet to teeter by.

They have wrinkles and weariness

vu s'écrouler son adolescence a accepté sans sourciller l'écroulement de sa dignité.

Les puceaux d'ici, portent en eux une promesse de décrépitude masquée sous un ricanement.

Ils usurpent déjà cette grimace du meurtrier qui attend au coin de la rue, le couteau de la faim entre les dents, le passage d'un portefeuille qui se balancerait sur deux jambes.

Ils ont les rides et la lassitude

in their hearts, like a girl has a guy under her skin.

They mustn't smile, but sadly beg on bended knee, from men, some extra consolation.

Though these are little parrots who don't wish to owe anybody anything.

We all think we're somebody, ever since compulsory primary schooling was introduced.

With a diploma, everyone acquired the right to vote, along with

dans le coeur, comme une fille a un homme dans la peau.

Ils ne devraient pas sourire, mais, tristement demander à genoux, aux hommes, le pourboire de quelques consolations.

Mais ce sont de petits perroquets qui ne veulent rien devoir à quiconque.

Nous nous croyons tous quelqu'un, depuis l'introduction de l'école primaire obligatoire.

Avec le certificat d'études scolaire, tout homme a acquis le droit au vote, à la

huge
self-regard and a lofty solitude.

No one, no one wants to live happily anymore; and who would want to give up on understanding life, to give it up for nothing?

Here, the sun never looks like the head of a bird killed by a lightning bolt, but moves around the red stools in one café or the round tables in another.

grande
considération de soi-même, et à la haute solitude.

Nul, nul ne veut plus vivre heureux; et qui voudrait renoncer à comprendre la vie pour la donner gratuitement?

Ici, le soleil n'a jamais l'aspect d'une tête d'oiseau tué d'un coup de foudre, mais promène la rondeur des tabourets rouges d'un café ou des tables rondes d'un autre.

Everyone's corruptible, but not my neighborhood.

It's the diamond no gangster would filch, not even the perpetrator of the theft of the Begum's jewels. This bullet-holed beauty's spoiling in the sun, godless, with a church full of atheists, alongside police headquarters in the sixth district.

My neighborhood, a ring on the finger of Paris.

My starry neighborhood, why didn't they build the Arc de Triomphe

Tous les hommes sont corruptibles, mais mon quartier ne l'est pas.

C'est le diamant qu'aucun gangster ne dérobera, fut-il l'auteur du vol des bijoux de la Bégum. Cette belle fusillée pourrit au soleil, sans dieu, avec toute une église d'athées, aux côtés du commissariat de police du sixième arrondissement.

Quartier, bague au doigt de Paris.

Quartier étoile, pourquoi n'a-t-on pas construit l'arc de triomphe

on your spine?

No doubt because the spirit never triumphs, no?

Who still has the courage to try living, when no one's afraid of dying anymore?

Solitude isn't a vocation.

It's to be earned, like death, through years of mortification and gangrene, through cozy chats with sin

sur ton échine?

Sans doute est-ce, parce qu'il n'y a pas de triomphe de l'esprit?

Qui a encore le courage de tenter de vivre, quand personne n'a plus peur de mourir?

La solitude n'est pas une vocation.

Elle se gagne comme la mort par des années de mortification et de gangrène, par des tête à tête avec le péché

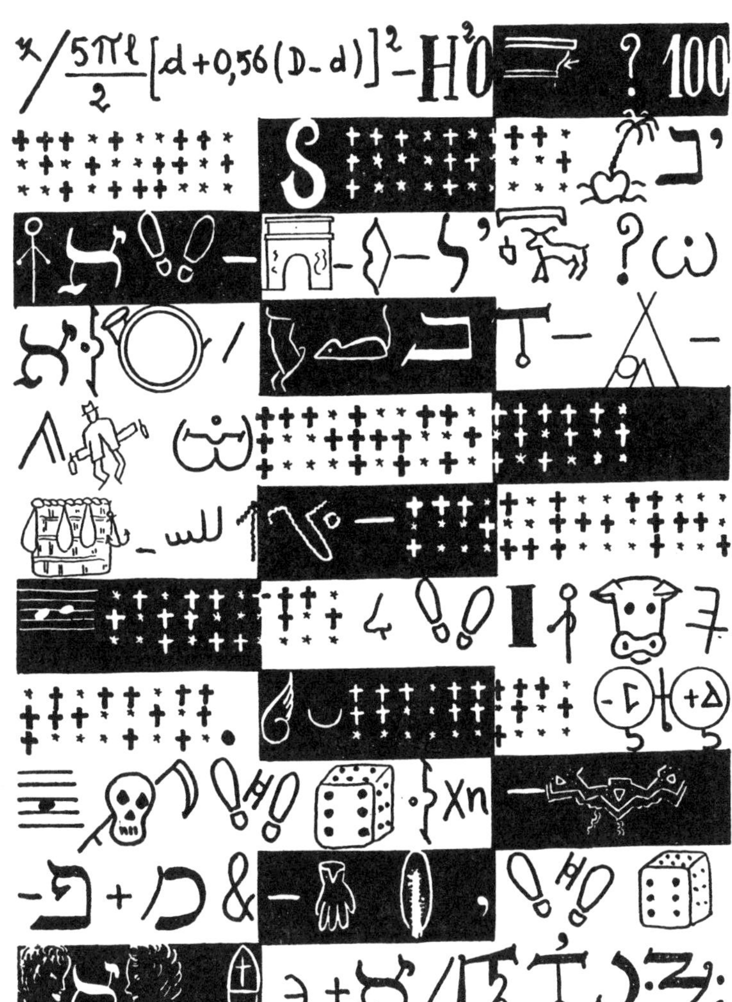

and outbursts at its accomplices.

This neighborhood ought to be torn up like Marseilles' streets of ill repute during the German occupation.

A new mob shoves a smart knife into the bellies of men who take their meals three times a day and their wives but once a week.

For sure a snitch will show up some night to spy on the neighborhood for the prefecture

et des coups de tête vers ses complices.

Il faudrait raser ce quartier comme les rues mal famées de Marseille pendant l'occupation allemande.

Une nouvelle pègre joue du couteau de l'intelligence dans le ventre des hommes qui prennent leurs repas trois fois par jour et leur femme une seule fois par semaine.

Il faudrait qu'un mouchard se ramène une nuit et carfarde le quartier à la préfecture

of police.

The whole neighborhood of underground clubs, of intellectual whores, of pull-out pricks, of novelizing midwives, of little degenerates who lap up jitterbug and jazz bands.

We must hang sound poets.

They pound our language so it bounds around to the point where we can't tell anymore if we're in Paris or Siberia.

de police.

Tout le quartier des beuglants souterrains, des putains intellectuelles, des onanistes semi-avortés, des sages-femmes romancières, des petits vicieux qui lapent du jitterbug et du jazz-band.

Il faut pendre les poètes onomatopéiques.

Ils dérouillent notre langue qui est gazelle au point qu'on ne sait plus si nous sommes à Paris ou en Sibérie.

We must hang these poets who rule here like monarchs, who've turned this neighborhood into a Babel of languages.

One of these nights, fire trucks and police cars will pull up, drawn by the sirens' songs.

While processions of dragons and alligators, which infest the neighborhood, will be arrested on the spot and shot immediately without a hearing for having attacked men's mugs, which they mashed up with guitars and cow-fish, a species invented by this neighborhood so as to cloud vision.

And the

Il faut pendre ces poètes qui règnent ici en maîtres, et qui ont fait de ce quartier la Tour de Babel des langues.

Une nuit, des chars de pompiers et des voitures de police s'amèneront, portés par les cris des sirènes.

Tandis que dragons et alligators en série, qui infestent le quartier, seront arrêtés sur place et fusillés sur le champ sans jugement préalable, pour attentat sur la gueule des hommes qu'ils ont incorporés aux guitares et aux poissons-vaches, race inventée par le quartier pour le brouillage des yeux.

Et les

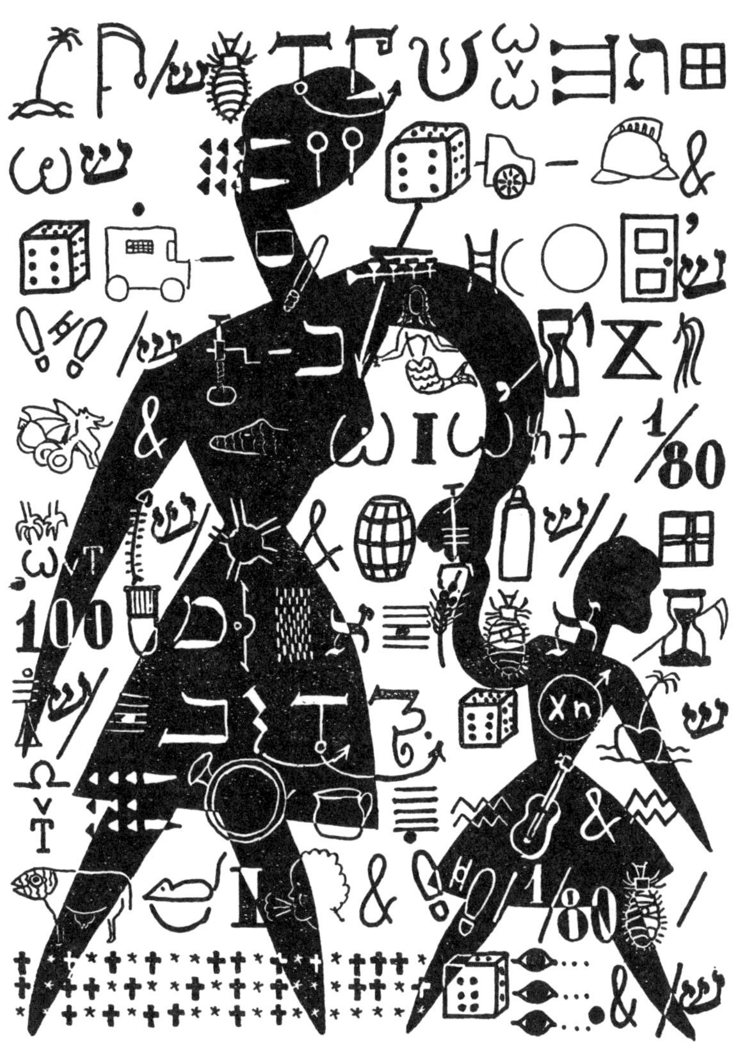

girls, whom France needs to reproduce itself, will be relentlessly pursued.

Slender cyclists will be snatched, and gallantly mounted on machines specially turned from back to front.

And they'll no longer know an asshole from a cunt.

And day by day they'll discover that they're men, though they'd been taken for women, just as

filles, dont la France a besoin pour la reproduction des siens seront chassées à coups de talon.

On prendra les petits pédaleurs, et chevaleresquement on les enfourchera sur des machines de spécifique transformation du derrière en avant.

Et ils ne sauront plus distinguer l'oeil du cul de l'oeil du truc.

Et ils se découvriront hommes d'un jour à l'autre, bien qu'on les ait pris pour femmes, comme

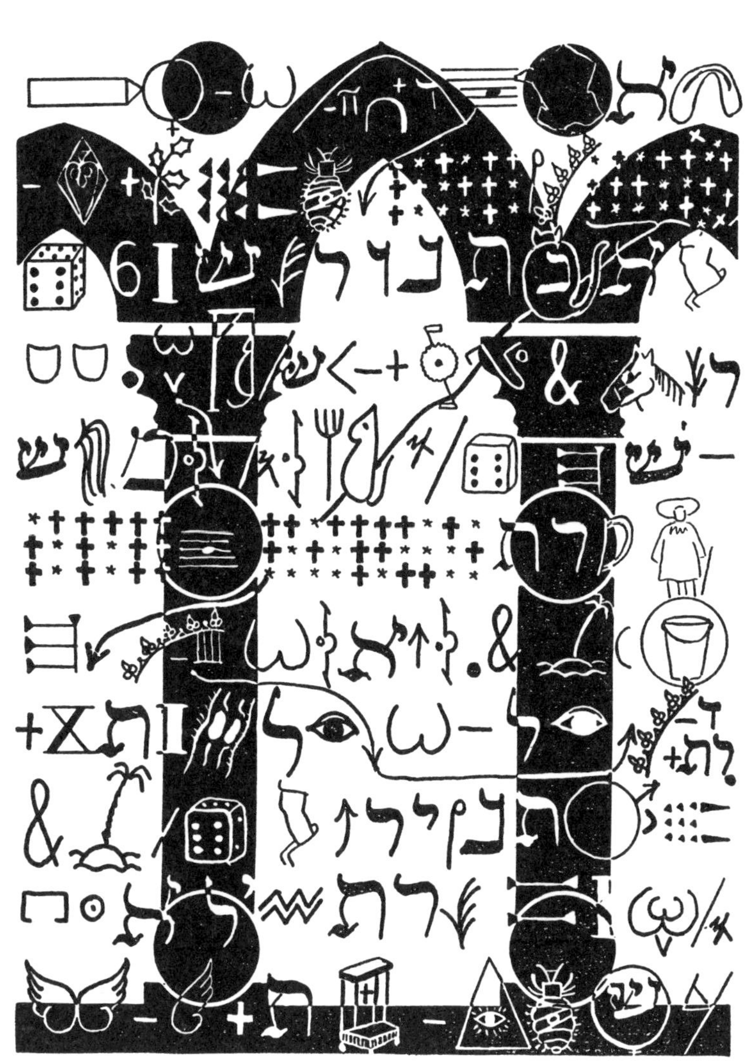

before, they'd understood themselves to be women while looking like men.

Thus they'll become fake men having been fake women who thought themselves real.

Men or women, they'll whirl within the misunderstanding nudged forward in the awkwardness of lust, after having whirled within the misunderstanding of the senses, without finding a way out through their pleasure holes,

autrefois ils eurent la révélation d'être des femmes bien qu'ayant l'aspect des hommes.

Ainsi deviendront-ils de faux hommes ayant été de fausses femmes qui se prenaient pour vraies.

Ils ou elles tourbillonneront dans le malentendu poussé un peu plus avant dans la maladresse de la luxure, après avoir tourbillonné dans le malentendu des sens, sans découvrir de sortie par leurs trous à plaisirs,

while having one too many.

We must plug all the holes in the neighborhood.

Holes of the spirit, holes of the cellars and the rats, saxophone holes, hooker holes, and the fake holes of virgins, and holes in the immense sky, itself a terrifying bullet hole, through which all that hemorrhages from this neighborhood ran in a single night.

All the blood from these streets' veins ran toward the Seine, leaving on the Paris map this bloodless corner, pale as if crucified.

We must find the culprit who cut

en ayant un de trop.

Il faut boucher tous les trous du quartier.

Les trous de l'esprit, les trous des caves et des rats, les trous des saxophones, les trous des putains, et les faux trous des pucelles, et les trous de ce ciel immense qui est un trou de balle terrible, par lequel toute l'hémorragie de ce quartier s'est écoulée en une seule nuit.

Tout le sang des veines de ces rues s'est écoulé vers la Seine, en laissant sur la carte de Paris, ce coin exsangue, pâle comme un crucifié.

Il faudrait trouver le coupable qui a tranché

the first groove, and capped the knee.

No doubt it's not simply the good lord who stuck the knife of the church in the lungs of Saint germain des prés.

But someday the police will come and the good lord will be carted off in a van and thrown in prison with riff-raff, assassins, and crooks.

We'll demand that firefighters eliminate leprosy from Paris, its mysteries, and Saint germain des prés.

We'll

la première entaille, et donné le coup de jarret dans le genou.

Sans doute n'est-ce tout simplement que le bon dieu, qui a planté le poignard de l'église dans les poumons de Saint germain de prés.

Mais, un jour, la police viendra, et le bon dieu sera cafardé aux hirondelles, et il sera foutu en prison avec les assassins, les fripouilles et les escrocs.

On demandera aux pompiers de saccager la lèpre de Paris, ses mystères, et Saint germain des prés.

On leur

demand that they restore the visible desert to the actual desert, so no one's mistaken anymore and so no one gets lost anymore in these crypt-like twists and turns, and so no one goes mad, like me, in this cemetery.

Besides, there is no Saint germain des prés.

There's only scenery.

Go out on the streets at night and you'll see nothing but cardboard, papier-mâché mansions, where manikins, manipulated on fragile

demandera de rendre le désert visible au désert réel, afin qu'on ne s'y trompe plus et qu'on ne s'égare plus dans ces dédales qui sont autant de cryptes, et qu'on ne devienne pas fou, comme moi, dans ce cimetière.

D'ailleurs, il n'y a pas de Saint germain des prés.

Il n'y a que des décors.

Sortez la nuit, dans les rues, et vous verrez qu'il n'y a que du carton-pâte, des maisons en papier-mâché, où des mannequins, tirés par des ficelles

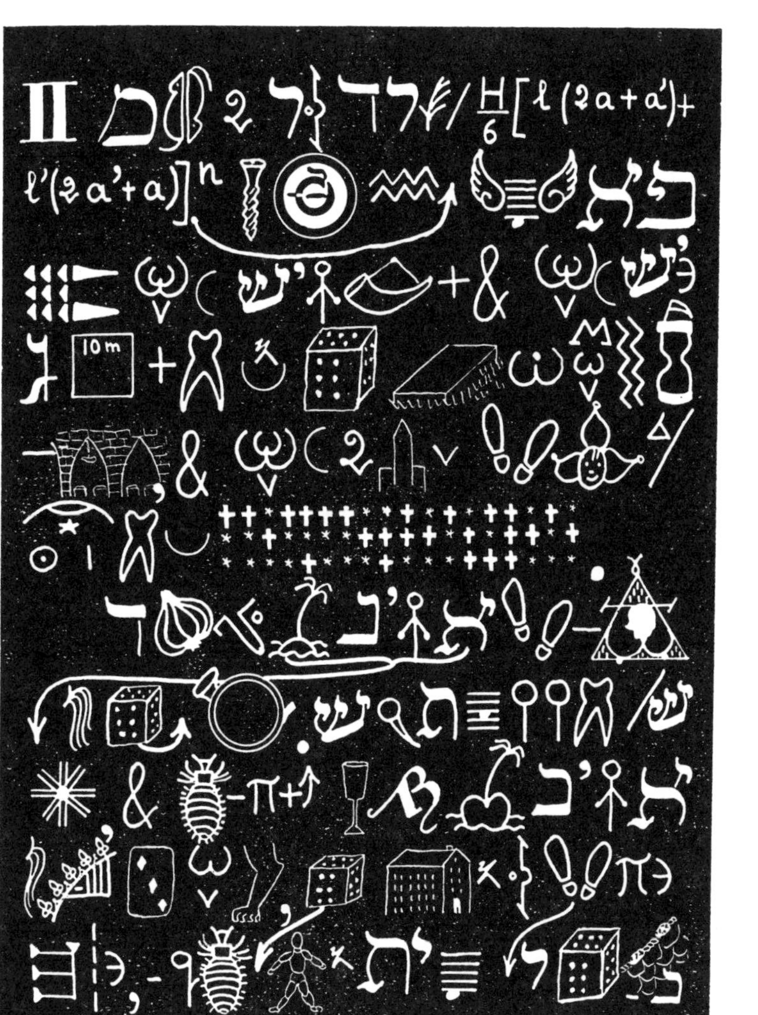

wires, spout water and urine on the heads of night owls who come visiting.

Saint germain des prés is like Donogoo-Tonga,[18] *a neighborhood specially built for the needs of foreign clients – like Venice for American tourists – for the currency needs of the temporarily insolvent French Republic.*

Come firefighters. Come machinists.

Carry off the scenery of Saint germain des prés.

You see, there's no

fragiles, jettent de l'eau et de l'urine à la tête des noctambules qui sont venus en visiteurs.

Saint germain des prés, est comme Donogoo-Tonga, un quartier bâti ad-hoc, pour les besoins de la clientèle étrangère — comme Venise pour les américains de passage — pour les besoins en devises de la république française provisoirement fauchée.

Venez pompiers. Venez machinistes.

Enlevez le décor de Saint germain de prés.

Vous voyez, il n'y a plus per

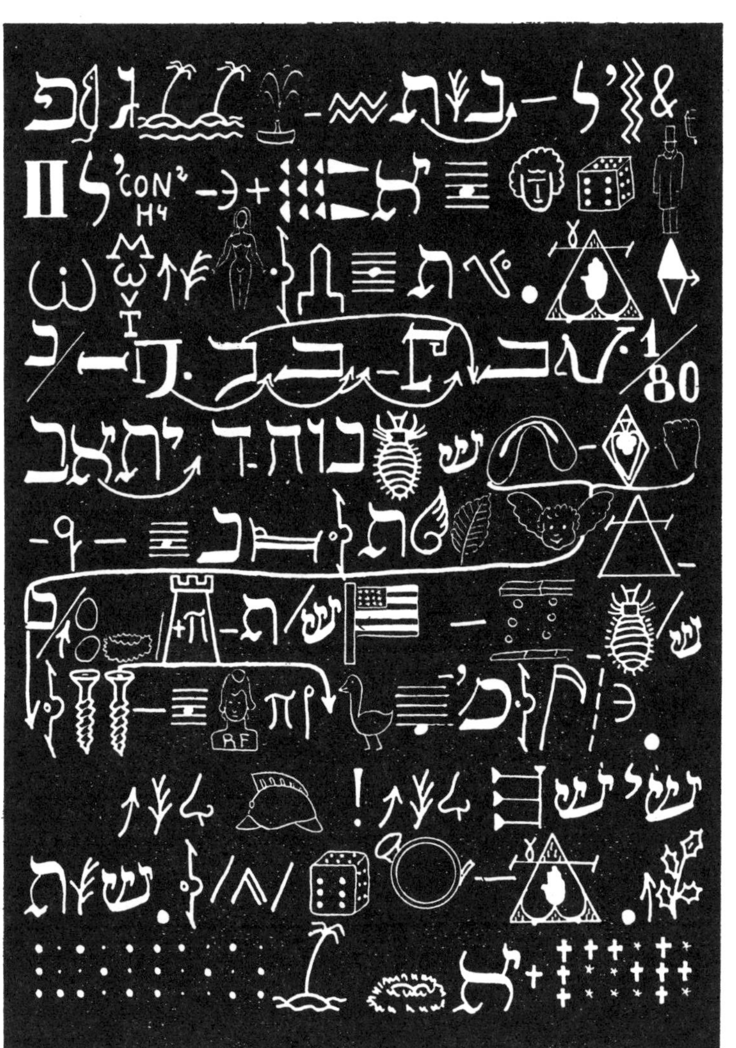

one left, no one, but me, down on my luck, all alone like a dog howling at death in the solitude of an empty desert.

Paris, August 20, 1949

sonne, plus personne, que moi, dans la dèche, tout solitaire comme un chien hurlant à la mort dans la solitude d'un désert vide.

Paris, le 20 août 1949

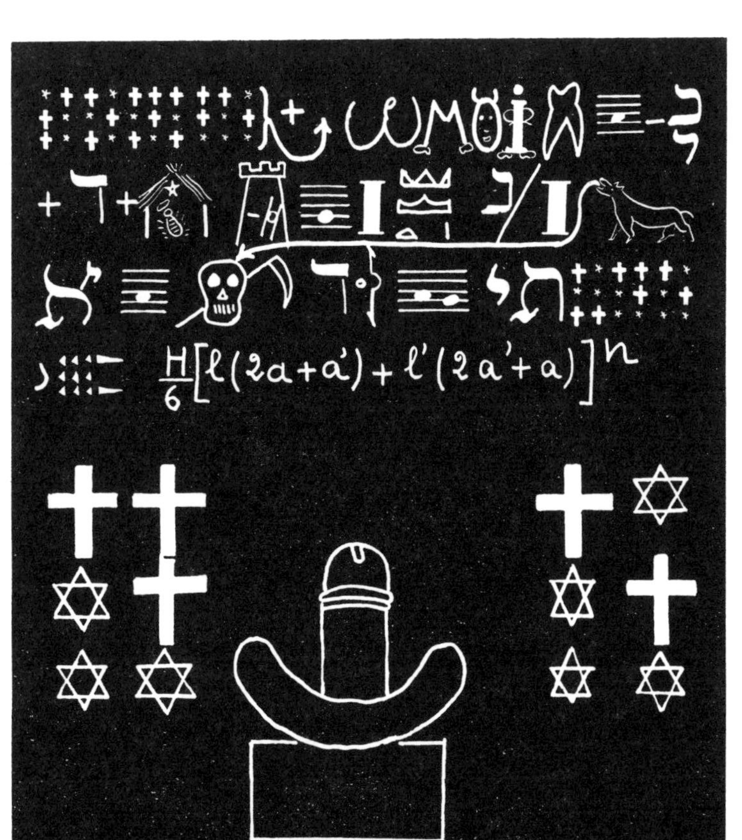
$\frac{H}{6}\left[l(2a+a')+l'(2a'+a)\right]^n$
Gabriel Pomerand

Author's Record[19]

Literature

The cry and its archangel or *the evolution of an ex-student.* (Édit. Fontaine.)

A bastard's meditations or *the entertainments of an archangel.* (Presses Littéraires de France.)

Open letters on a myth or *the childishness of a bashful lover.* (Under contract.)

Nota bene or *the testament of a disappointed archangel.* (In press.)

Notes on prostitution or *worldly remarks on a profound subject.* (1950.)

The intimate diary of a notorious sex-fiend, followed by his works. (Forthcoming.)

Little immemorial on imperfection or *the art of appreciating ignorance.* (In progress.)

Autobiography of Mephistopheles or *the misfortunes of a convert.* (In progress.)

Leaves for an intimate enemy or *open letters to my best friend.* (Forthcoming.)

Narrative of the grotto of Totis or *the abortions of knowledge.* (In progress.)

Ten lectures delivered. (In progress.)

Saint ghetto of the loans or *Paris, your décor is passé!* [20]

Theater

The devil's bistro or *the misunderstandings of love.* (Play in three acts. — In progress.)

The trial of a cynic or *Diogenes smiles.* (Play in three acts. — In progress.)

A million cuckolds. (Vaudeville in one act. — In progress.)

Dance

The man who would build his own tomb or *a debased lesson in interpretation*, pantomime. (In progress.)

Ten untitled ballets. (In progress.)

Music

Nineteen onomatopoeic oratorios. (Forthcoming.)

Eight scores for percussion instruments.

Cinema

The symbolism of tattoos (Cinematographic commentary.)

Perfect Pépin amongst the people. (Scenario. — In Progress.)

Monsieur Banal seeks his double. (Scenario. — In Progress.)

Notes to the Text

The identifications below of names indicated by x*'s in the text are, in some cases, just guesses. (MK)*

1 Boris Vian (1920–1959), novelist, playwright, critic, jazz musician.

2 Raymond Queneau (1903–1976), experimental novelist and poet, essayist, editor.

3 *I Spit on Your Graves* (*J'irai cracher sur vos tombes*, Paris, 1946), a best-selling noir novel, originally passed off as a translation from the American, by Vian.

4 With all its *x*'s decrypted, this line might translate as "Boris Vian, sort of a current Kobra, scorpion man." Maurice Dekobra (sometimes spelled "de Kobra," 1885–1973) was a popular novelist; Vian's *J'irai cracher...* was published by Éditions du Scorpion. (Thanks to Jean-Louis Rançon for correcting my previous interpretation, and to Jan Baetens for additional advice.)

5 Jean-Paul Sartre (1905–1980), leading Existentialist philosopher, novelist, etc.

6 Unknown word.

7 Alexandre Astruc (1923–2016), filmmaker, critic.

8 Cazalis dixit Anne-Marie = Anne-Marie Cazalis (1920–1988), actress, singer, journalist, novelist, grand-niece of Henri Cazalis (1840–1909), Mallarmé's friend.

9 Anne.

10 Marie Cazalis.

11 Astruc.

12 Gréco = Juliette Gréco (1927–2020), actress, singer.

13 Uncertain identification. Perhaps Marc Doelnitz (1921–2000), actor, costume designer; perhaps Pomerand himself.

14 Unknown word.

15 Camus = Albert Camus (1913–1960), novelist, essayist.

16 Jean-Isidore = Isidore Isou.

17 Claude Mauriac (1914–1996), novelist, essayist.

18 *Donogoo-Tonka* by Jules Romains (1885–1972), an early screenplay-novel (1919) about a concocted city in South America.

19 The "Author's Record" is Pomerand's own list of his works, printed at the back of the original edition.

20 "*Paris, your décor is passé!*" is a phrase from Jacques Baratier's movie *Le Désordre* (*Disorder*). See Translator's Afterword and the Bibliography & Filmography below.

Translator's Afterword

WHEN THE FIRST VERSION of this translation came out in 2006, *Saint ghetto des prêts* was little known, even in France. It had been out of print and out of sight since 1950, although pages had been reproduced occasionally in exhibition catalogs and critical studies (including Greil Marcus's *Lipstick Traces*). Reissuing a complete *Saint Ghetto* was, and is again, meant to make more widely available one of the seminal and most accomplished among a large body of verbo-visual work from the Lettrist movement in post–World War II Paris. If Lettrists are remembered at all today, it's usually their theorizing about total art and social transformation that's emphasized—often in relation to the group's more renowned offshoot, Situationism—rather than their artifacts.

In the original, French edition of *Saint ghetto des prêts*, the text was probably linotyped, and zinc blocks used for the rebuses. Its pages were 29 cm (11½") high by 22.5 cm (8⅞") wide. Though much smaller in size, the current edition attempts to represent as closely as possible the typesetting of Pomerand's prose-poem paragraphs, its margins and indentations, some of its idiosyncratic hyphenations, and intentionally jarring page breaks.

The relationship between the images and the French text is the witty heart of the book. Little footprints, for instance, "pas" in French, regularly stand for the word's homonym, the negative participle "pas"; the formula "H_2O"—water is "eau" in French, pronounced like the English-language letter 'O'—is used when that sound is part of a word.

All of that makes reading delightful but translating an almost ridiculous exercise. Nonetheless, translation enables those who know no French to experience the narrative, a prose poem about life in the liberated, bohemian Left Bank. The title, "Saint Ghetto of the Loans," is a play on another name for the neighborhood, derived from that of its old abbey: Saint-Germain-des-Prés (Saint Germain of the Fields).

"Grimoire"

IN FRENCH, THE BOOK'S subtitle is not merely a manual of magic, as it is in English, but may also refer to an obscure language, or an illegible scrawl.

Rebuses

A REBUS—WHICH CAN BE simple or ingeniously complicated—uses pictures and symbols to suggest syllables, words, or phrases. Decoding the message requires guesswork and provides entertainment.

Though clearly related to ancient hieroglyphs, rebuses, in the modern sense of wordplay, date to Classical Greece where they were used in carvings and on coins. In the Middle Ages they appeared in illuminated manuscripts and later in heraldic designs, and in the Renaissance in esoteric literary satires. By the eighteenth century they'd become an upper-class parlor game, then spread throughout Europe and the New World in the bourgeois nineteenth, as literacy rates rose.

Pomerand's rebuses don't function as puzzles, strictly speaking, since he reveals the texts represented by the pictograms. But his representations are so complicated readers would be at quite a loss if he didn't, and anyway, matching the words and pictures remains challenging and fun. Provided one knows a little French.

The dazzling layouts are sometimes helpful in deciphering the images, sometimes not. For the first dozen or so pages, the images run left to right, like ordinary text. In the next dozen, lines start running backwards or at angles, sometimes with arrows indicating the narrative's direction. Thereafter, the pattern becomes text-like again, but interwoven with bold graphics, more and more dramatically exploring reversals, white on black, until, near the end, each page is altogether reversed. Throughout, the pictographic sentences have some punctuation, corresponding to the prose poem's, and that's one major guidepost for interpretation.

Lettrism

AFTER WORLD WAR II, Paris tried to resume its place in world culture. Resistance writers surfaced from underground, exiled Surrealists returned, and youth groups like the Existentialists and Lettrists emerged to produce a whirlwind of performances, exhibits, and publications in and around the cafés of Saint-Germain-des-Prés.

Lettrism ("lettrisme" in French, and sometimes "Letterism" in English) was founded in 1945, when Isidore Isou (real name Jean-Isidore Goldstein), a twenty-year-old Romanian refugee, met Pomerand in a Saint-Germain soup kitchen for Jewish orphans. Isou, precocious, had already begun formulating his aesthetic—a philosophy of constant creative renewal in which, among other things, letterforms were to be the basis, the underlying principle, of future artwork, superseding abstraction as abstraction had displaced figuration. Pomerand became his "first disciple and friend."[1] He was a perfect match for Isou's theorizing: a gifted practitioner. With several others, they soon expanded their libertarian and mixed-media notions into a full-fledged art movement: publishing polemics; displaying paintings; performing sound poetry in the clubs (both startling and hilarious, according to eyewitnesses); organizing provocative public lectures on, for instance, prostitution, and pederasty; writing endlessly about films, and making radically short ones. Whatever they did, they did in defiant, anti-establishment ways, and they always sought and got lots of press attention. They played a big part in the first postwar counterculture.

In addition, their focus on the graphic nature of writing had a more directly artistic impact—on visual literature in the Sixties and after. "Metagraphics" is what Isou, Pomerand, and Maurice Lemaître, then a recent recruit, first labeled the rebus style that all three employed in competing text/image projects in 1949. The end results (each to some extent remindful of Raymond Queneau's "Pictogrammes," which had appeared in print not long before)[2] were:

• 50 visual pages in Isou's *Diaries of the Gods* (smaller in format than *Saint Ghetto*, with some of the glyphs drawn by Lemaître, and preceded by a critical essay—"...On the Definition, Evolution, and Total Overhaul of Prose and the Novel"—four times as long);

• Lemaître's own ten plates, entitled "Riff-raff," in his magazine *Ur*;

• and *Saint Ghetto*, the only one of the three to have a textual key to the rebuses.

Together, they mark the starting point for decades of exciting Lettrist page design, by Lemaître, who continued creating what he renamed "hypergraphics," and by Roland Sabatier, Roberto Altmann, and Alain Satié, among others.

Although Isou's "metagraphic" work was the one that actually appeared in print first, in the spring of 1950, Pomerand's was the most original, fully achieved, amusing, and beautiful of the three, and a high point in the history of artists' books.

Pomerand

POMERAND WAS BORN ON June 13, 1925, in Paris. After his father died in 1929, he and his mother moved to Alsace, where he attended both Jewish and communal schools. In 1939, they were evacuated to Marseilles. As a lycée student, during the war, Gabriel worked in the Resistance. His mother was deported to Auschwitz.[3] He survived somehow and what's more discovered Nietzsche, Rimbaud, and Lautréamont in this period, so when at the end of the war he made his way to Paris and met Isou, he was ready.

Pomerand's was the public face of Lettrism in its first years. An intentionally scandalous face. He was sued for defamation, jailed for brawling, and on several occasions arrested for affronts to public morality (obscenity, nudity). With his slight frame, frizzy hair, and (when dressed) downscale fashion sense, he was a mainstay at the famous Club Tabou, where his sound poetry was celebrated. Boris Vian wrote, "Pomerand was one of the most surprising individuals at Tabou... He had a special, confrontational way of reciting his lettrist works, and you wondered at any moment whence he drew his voice, and whether it would stay there for another word."[4] Isou described Pomerand's life at that time as "made up of days of ferocious hunger and nights homeless under the bridges—mixed with windfalls of wealth and luxury thanks to the aristocratic moneybags among whom this 'Angel Gabriel' strode with ceremonial charm and superior disdain."[5] Other income apparently came from fencing books that Jean Genet filched from stalls along the Seine, and contributions from better-heeled friends, Juliette Gréco and Jean-Paul Sartre among them.

Saint Ghetto began in 1947 as the voice-over commentary for a documentary by Jacques Baratier[6] about the Left Bank scene. The text was completed in mid-1949, as noted by Pomerand in the book; then the visuals were created—following epigraphic research at the Bibliothèque Nationale, and with assistance from his artist friends Aline Gagnaire and Bernard Quentin[7]—using the recently introduced ballpoint pen.[8] By that time Pomerand knew he had tuberculosis, and he was already pulling away from the Lettrist group, his relations with Isou turning sour. In December, he converted to Greek Catholicism in order to marry Roxane Chiniara (to whom *Saint Ghetto* is dedicated), the daughter of Egyptian King Farouk's insurance agent; after their extravagant wedding in Cairo on February 2, 1950, he had to hurry back to Paris for a court date on a charge of pornography. In August, *Saint Ghetto* was issued in an edition of 440, for sale by subscription at 1,000 francs ($2.85) a copy.

Although largely forgotten now, Pomerand's work was influential, in an underground way. He's credited with broaching the psycho-geographical notion of the "dérive" (later elaborated by Guy Debord) in *A Bastard's Meditations, or The Entertainments of an Archangel* (1949).[9] His sound art—notably *La Symphonie en K*[10]—spawned decades of "poésie sonore," and his short *La Légende cruelle*, about Leonor Fini, won first prize at the French film awards in 1951. He also did oil paintings, featuring hermetic notations similar to some in *Saint Ghetto*,[11] which hung regularly in Lettrist exhibitions over the years, even though he was periodically expelled from the movement, in 1952 as a "falsifier" and "nonentity," and in 1956 for "indolence." That, despite his having brought out, by then, at least five books. Afterward: prolific periodical publication (cultural criticism, pseudonymous book reviews); assorted short films; opium addiction; a roman à clef: *Les Puérils*, published by Robert Laffont in 1956; some hard-to-describe limited editions; world travel... then, worsening health, cared for by Juliette Gréco... psychedelics in New York in early 1966 (his reflections on L.S.D. issued later that year by Christian Bourgois as *Le D. man*). He died in Paris on June 26, 1972.

Notes:

1 Roland Sabatier, *Le Lettrisme, les créations et les créateurs* (Z'éditions, 1989), p. 55.

2 In *Messages*, nos. 1–2 (1946), no page numbers.

3 Personal communication, from M. Jacques Donguy.

4 Boris Vian, *Manuel de Saint-Germain-des-Prés* (Éditions du Chêne, 1974), p. 209.

5 Isidore Isou, "Les Grandes poètes lettristes" in *Bizarre*, nos. 32–33 (1964), p. 68.

6 An 18-minute version of *Disorder*, featuring Pomerand and Juliette Gréco, among others, was released in 1950. Online, 1/7/23, at https://www.youtube.com/watch?v=cXbokkOs3oY.

7 François Letaillieur, *Gabriel Pomerand* (Galerie 1900-2000, 2004), no page numbers.

8 Letaillieur, "Gabriel Pomerand, le cri légendaire de Saint-Germain-des-Prés" in *Supérieur inconnu*, no. 6 (1997), p. 80.

9 ibid., p. 78. The cited line from *Bastard's Meditations* (no page number provided) translates as "The pot-bellied one is divine but from the moment change channels itself toward *drift [se canalise vers la dérive], the babbling loses itself in mystery, the community wanders toward a sigh, and imprecation, sign of God, turns into blasphemy, which frames the man with billy goat heels.*" [Pomerand's italics]

10 For an extract from the score, see *La Revue musicale*, nos. 282–283 (1971), no page numbers.

11 Reproductions in Letaillieur, *Le Demi-siècle lettriste* (Galerie 1900-2000, 1988), p. 60 ff.

Gabriel Pomerand: Bibliography & Filmography

{compiled by M. Kasper}

Books

Le Cri et son archange: contradiction entre un bâtard et son archange, ou L'Évolution d'un exmatriculé. Paris, Fontaine, 1948.
—Reprint: Andeville, Cahiers de L'Externité, 1998.

Lettres ouvertes à un Mythe, ou Les Enfantillages d'un amoureux transi. Geneva, Aux dépens d'un amateur [self-published], 1949.

Le Testament d'un archange déçu. [Paris, self-published], 1949.

Considérations objectives sur la pédérastie: conférence interdite par le préfet de police, les sexes mal famés. Paris, Aux dépens du public [self-published], 1949.
—Reprint (a): Lille, Cahiers Gai-Kitsch-Camp, 1995.
—Reprint (b): in *Conférences.* Andeville, Cahiers de L'Externité, 1998.

Les Méditations d'un bâtard, ou Les Divertissements d'un archange. Paris, Presses Littéraires de France, 1949.

Notes sur la prostitution. Paris, Aux dépens de la morale [self-published], 1950.
—Reprint: in *Conférences.* Andeville, Cahiers de L'Externité, 1998.

Saint ghetto des prêts: grimoire. Paris, O.L.B., 1950.
—Translated into English as *Saint Ghetto of the Loans: Grimoire*. Brooklyn, Ugly Duckling Presse, 2006
—"Amplified edition," New York, World Poetry Books, 2023.

Le Testament d'un acquitté, précédé de Ses aveux publics. Paris, René Julliard, 1951.

Antonio: hors de galaxie. Paris, Jacques Loyau, 1954.

Les Puérils: roman. Paris, Robert Laffont, 1956.

Le Petit philosophie de poche. Paris, Librairie Générale Française / Livre de Poche, 1962.

Le D. Man. Paris, Christian Bourgois, 1966.
—Reprint: [Paris], Les Livres de Nulle Part, 1994.

Selected Periodical and Anthology Publications

"Pathétique sans râtelier: correspondance publique," pp. 52–56 in *La Dictature lettriste: cahiers d'un nouveau régime artistique* (1946).
—Reprint: Luzarches, Cahiers de L'Externité, 2000.

"Accouchement distillé des peureuses palmes"; "Complainte sur les rives de l'oeil multiple" by Pol Meyra (pseud.), pp. 7–8 in *Hikma* (no. 2, 1948).

"Trois suicides significatifs"; "L'Example de Franz Werfel," pp. 698–701 in *Psyché: revue internationale des sciences de l'homme et de psychanalyse* (no. 20, 1948).

"Lettre ouverte à mes créanciers pour arrêter une hémorragie de réclamations inopportunes," pp. 21–26 in *Osmose* (nos. 2–3, 1949).
—Reprint: Rouen, Éditions Derrière La Salle de Bains (Collection Acquaviva), 2008.

"Discours d'un terroriste," pp. 5–6 in *Ur* (no. 2, 1951).
—Reprint: in *Conférences.* Andeville, Cahiers de L'Externité, 1998.

"La Légende cruelle," pp. 159–166 in *Ion: centre de création* (1952).
—Reprint: Paris, Jean-Paul Rocher, 1999.

"Carmen Amaya," pp. 22–24 in *Revue chorégraphique de Paris* (May 1952).

"Ouverture en A, opus XXVI...," pp. 35–37 in *Ur* (no. 3, 1953).

"Chanson d'amour en un pays lointain"; "Son de cloches en leur fidélité," pp. 39–40 in *Revue lettriste et hypergraphique* (no. 1, 1959).

"Origine de l'humanisme," p. 57 in *Haute Société* (no. 2, 1960).

"Symphonie en K (extrait)," [unpaginated] in *La Revue musicale* (nos. 282–283, 1971).

Films

Le Désordre. Directed by Jacques Baratier. 18 mins., 1950. A 24-minute edit came out in 1966, with extra footage from the 1960s, entitled *Le Désordre à vingt ans.* In 2009, Baratier's daughter Diane assembled a third, 93-minute version, *Un Beau désordre.* Pomerand contributed to the concept, scenario, and soundtrack of the original, and performed. Online 1/7/23, at https://www.youtube.com/watch?v=cXbokkOs30Y.

La Légende cruelle. Directed by Pomerand and Arcady Brachlianof. 25 mins., 1951.

La Peau du milieu (Les Tatoués du bout du monde). Written and directed by Pomerand. 14 mins., 1957. Online, 1/7/23, at https://www.youtube.com/watch?v=rX9BeVGUldk.

Reproductions of Paintings

- in *Le Soulèvement de la jeunesse* (pp. 8–9 in no. 1, 1952; pp. 8–9 in no. 2, 1952; pp. 8–9 in no. 3, 1952).

- in *Le Demi-siècle lettriste* by François Lettaillieur. Paris, Galerie 1900-2000, 1988, pp. 60–65.

- in *La Peinture lettriste* by Isidore Isou, Alain Satié, and Gérard Bermond. Paris, Jean-Paul Rocher, 2000, pp. 67–68.

- in *Gabriel Pomerand* by François Letaillieur (see below), plates III–VIII.

Secondary Sources

Guillaume Robin, "Gabriel Pomerand, la légende du siècle," chapter 8, pp. 275–314 in *Les Peintres oubliés: Du Quattrocento à l'ère moderne*. Nice, Les Éditions Ovadia, 2014.

François Letaillieur, *Gabriel Pomerand*. Paris, Galerie 1900-2000, 2004.

François Letaillieur, "Gabriel Pomerand, le cri légendaire de Saint-Germain-des-Prés," pp. 67–91 in *Supérieur inconnu* (no. 6, 1997).

Acknowledgments

Thanks to Jan Baetens, Bob Bezucha, and Steve Heim for help and encouragement; to Matvei Yankelevich for artful editing and perseverance; to Jean-Louis Rançon for correcting an error in the first edition; to Aiden Farrell, C. Francis Fisher, Henry Gifford, and Jocelyn Spaar for their careful and insightful readings; to Ryan Haley for his work on the first edition of this translation for Ugly Duckling Presse in 2006; and to Garance Pomerand for her permission to republish this work. —*M.K.*

In 1945, after several years in the French Resistance, **Gabriel Pomerand** (1925–1972) returned to Paris where, together with Romanian refugee Isidore Isou, he launched the Lettrist movement, catalyzing a loose collective of avant-garde writers, visual artists, filmmakers, and cabaret performers in Left Bank Paris. There Pomerand organized scandalous public lectures, gave performances of sound poetry, painted oils, and made an award-winning short movie. His prolific output over the years included innovative artists books and novels, as well as screenplays, cultural criticism, and book reviews.

Michael Kasper is an essayist and maker of a dozen artists books. He has also translated work by Belgian Surrealists Paul Nougé, Louis Scutenaire, and Paul Colinet, and German avant-garde visionary Paul Scheerbart, among others.

Bhamati Viswanathan is an independent legal scholar and the author of Cultivating Copyright: How Creative Industries Can Harness Intellectual Property to Survive the Digital Age (Routledge/Taylor & Francis). She works to empower artists of color both at home and in the developing world.

This book is typeset in Garamond Premier, designed by Robert Slimbach for Adobe in 2005, based on the sixteenth-century metal punches of Claude Garamond held at the Plantin-Moretus Museum in Antwerp. Titles and numbers are set in Le Jeune, designed by Paul Barnes, Christian Schwartz, and Greg Gazdowicz for Commercial Type.

The cover design is by Andrew Bourne based on the original cover by Gabriel Pomerand; the hand lettering is by Michael Kasper. Typeset by Don't Look Now. Printed and bound in Lithuania by BALTO print.

Jean-Paul Auxeméry
Selected Poems
tr. Nathaniel Tarn

Maria Borio
Transparencies
tr. Danielle Pieratti

Jeannette L. Clariond
Goddesses of Water
tr. Samantha Schnee

Jacques Darras
John Scotus Eriugena at Laon
tr. Richard Sieburth

Olivia Elias
Chaos, Crossing
tr. Kareem James Abu-Zeid

Phoebe Giannisi
Homerica
tr. Brian Sneeden

Zuzanna Ginczanka
On Centaurs and Other Poems
tr. Alex Braslavsky

Nakedness Is My End:
Poems from the Greek Anthology
tr. Edmund Keeley

Jazra Khaleed
The Light That Burns Us
ed. Karen Van Dyck

Dimitra Kotoula
The Slow Horizon that Breathes
tr. Maria Nazos

Jerzy Ficowski
Everything I Don't Know
tr. Jennifer Grotz & Piotr Sommer
PEN AWARD FOR POETRY IN TRANSLATION

Antonio Gamoneda
Book of the Cold
tr. Katherine M. Hedeen &
Víctor Rodríguez Núñez

Mireille Gansel
Soul House
tr. Joan Seliger Sidney

Óscar García Sierra
Houston, I'm the Problem
tr. Carmen Yus Quintero

Maria Laina
Hers
tr. Karen Van Dyck

Maria Laina
Rose Fear
tr. Sarah McCann

Perrin Langda
A Few Microseconds on Earth
tr. Pauline Levy Valensi

Manuel Maples Arce
Stridentist Poems
tr. KM Cascia

Enio Moltedo
Night
tr. Marguerite Feitlowitz

Meret Oppenheim
The Loveliest Vowel Empties:
Collected Poems
tr. Kathleen Heil

Elisabeth Rynell
Night Talks
tr. Rika Lesser

Giovanni Pascoli
Last Dream
tr. Geoffrey Brock
RAIZISS/DE PALCHI TRANSLATION AWARD

Gabriel Pomerand
Saint Ghetto of the Loans
tr. Michael Kasper &
Bhamati Viswanathan

Rainer Maria Rilke
Where the Paths Do Not Go
tr. Burton Pike

Waly Salomão
Border Fare
tr. Maryam Monalisa Gharavi

George Sarantaris
Abyss and Song: Selected Poems
tr. Pria Louka

Seo Jung Hak
The Cheapest France in Town
tr. Megan Sungyoon

Ardengo Soffici
Simultaneities & Lyric Chemisms
tr. Olivia E. Sears

Ye Lijun
My Mountain Country
tr. Fiona Sze-Lorrain

Paul Verlaine
Before Wisdom: The Early Poems
tr. Keith Waldrop & K. A. Hays

Uljana Wolf
kochanie, today i bought bread
tr. Greg Nissan

Verónica Zondek
Cold Fire
tr. Katherine Silver